The Reuther Brothers

Walter, Roy, and Victor

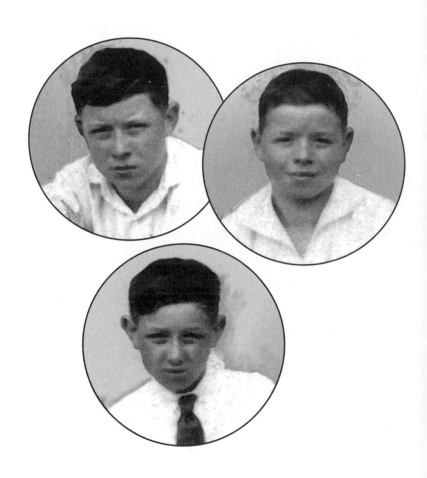

The Reuther Brothers

Walter, Roy, and Victor

MIKE AND PAM SMITH

WAYNE STATE UNIVERSITY PRESS   DETROIT

Great Lakes Books
Detroit Biography Series for Young Readers

First Lady of Detroit:
The Story of Marie-Thérèse Guyon, Mme Cadillac,
by Karen Elizabeth Bush, 2001

The Reuther Brothers—Walter, Roy, and Victor,
by Mike Smith and Pam Smith, 2001

Albert Kahn: Builder of Detroit,
by Roger Matuz, 2001

Willie Horton: Detroit's Own "Willie the Wonder,"
by Grant Eldridge and Karen Elizabeth Bush, 2001

Copyright © 2001 by Wayne State University Press, Detroit, Michigan 48201. All rights are reserved. No part of this book may be reproduced without formal permission. Manufactured in the United States of America.
05 04 03 02 01   5 4 3 2 1

Library of Congress Cataloging-in-Publication Data

Smith, Mike (Michael O.)
   The Reuther brothers : Walter, Roy, and Victor / Mike and Pam Smith.
      p. cm. — (Great lakes books) (Detroit biography series for young readers)
Includes index.
   ISBN 0-8143-2994-2 (alk. paper)   ISBN 0-8143-2995-0 (pbk. : alk. paper)
   1. Reuther, Walter, 1907-1970—Juvenile literature. 2. Reuther, Roy, 1909-1968—Juvenile literature. 3. Reuther, Victor G. (Victor George), 1912—Juvenile literature 4. Labor unions—United States—Officials and employees—Biography—Juvenile literature. 5. Labor leaders—United States—Biography—Juvenile literature. 6. Labor unions—Automobile industry workers—United States—History—Juvenile literature. 7. International Union, United Automobile, Aircraft, and Agricultural Implement Workers of America—History—Juvenile literature. [1. Reuther, Walter, 1907-1970. 2. Reuther, Roy, 1909-1968. 3. Reuther, Victor G. (Victor George), 1912- 4. Labor leaders.] I. Smith, Pam (Pamela V.) II. Title. III. Series. IV. Series: Detroit biography series for young readers
   HD6509.R4 S65 2001
   331.88'1292'092273—dc21

                         2001001688

All photographs are reproduced with the kind permission of the Walter P. Reuther Library, Wayne State University.

Designed by Mary Primeau

For our parents:
Owen and Joan, Harv and Gen

CONTENTS

1. The Stump *9*

2. Anna and Valentine *13*

3. Life in Wheeling *19*

4. Making Choices *23*

5. Going to Detroit *31*

6. The Depression *37*

7. The Big Adventure *45*

8. Exploring Europe *49*

9. Working in Gorky *53*

10. Building the UAW *59*

11. Sweethearts and Families *65*

12. The Reuther Legacy *69*

Epilogue *77*

Glossary *79*

Acknowledgments 83

❖ 1 ❖
The Stump

It was a hot, humid, sunny day and Walter's underwear itched. His family did not have much money this summer, so Walter had to wear underwear that his mother made from empty flour sacks. The sacks were soft and could be sewn into clothing, but he still didn't like them. His brothers, Roy and Victor, had to wear them, too. For a few years now, only the oldest brother, Ted, had new clothes—he had taken a job after he finished the eighth grade in school and needed to wear good clothes. When Ted outgrew his clothes, the other brothers would wear his shirts and pants until they also outgrew them.

But today, clothes did not matter. It was a glorious Saturday afternoon in West Virginia in 1922 and it was time to play.

The Reuther brothers had a special place to play. It was a patch of woods with a clearing in the middle. In the clearing was the stump of a huge tree—almost six feet across!

The stump was one of the Reuther brothers' favorite spots. It was special because this was where they practiced the art of giving speeches. From the stump, the brothers would debate the issues of the day. How many immigrants from other nations should the government allow into the United States? Was the president of the United States a good leader? Should all people be treated equally in America—especially black Americans?

Their father, Valentine Reuther, thought it was important for a person to be able to clearly express his or her ideas to other people. On Sundays, after the family finished dinner, he encouraged his children to debate the issues of the day. Father Reuther would pick a topic and ask each son to argue on one side of the issue. They would debate their father and each other for hours, learning the art of persuading others to listen to their ideas.

Tomorrow was Sunday—they must be prepared for the dinner-time discussion. "What topic do you think Dad will ask us to debate tomorrow?" Walter asked. Victor, the youngest, said: "Labor unions—that's his favorite thing to talk about." Roy agreed and jumped onto the stump: "Trade unions are good. People who work in mines, factories, stores, and warehouses, or those who build houses, unload ships, and drive delivery wagons, these workers should form a union. A trade union is formed when people who work in the same place and have similar skills join together to bargain as a group with the owner of the workplace for better work conditions, wages, and benefits. This is a good thing. It results in a contract or a deal between a business owner and his employees that is fair to both parties."

Roy jumped down and Walter hopped on the stump. Pretending he was a factory owner, Walter boldly stated: "I own the building where you work. I spend a lot of money to buy the machines and tools you use to make the products I must sell. I take great risks to make a successful business that provides many jobs for people in this city."

Not to be outdone, Roy jumped back onto the stump. Walter stayed there as well. Roy said: "But the workers in your factory are paid low wages, while you have a big house!" Walter replied: "I have a big house because I risked my money on the business and worked very hard. My success in business gives my workers steady jobs, and I pay them what I think I should." "Perhaps it is not enough," said Roy, thinking of his flour-sack underwear.

Victor decided to join his brothers on the stump. Remembering what Father Reuther had said many times, he declared loudly: "All people who work deserve dignity."

Just then, the brothers heard their mom, Anna, calling

them. Time to go. They decided they would finish the debate tomorrow and ran for home.

These three Reuther brothers, Walter, Roy, and Vic, stuck together for the rest of their lives. In the 1930s, many workers in America organized themselves into trade unions. The Reuther brothers decided to make their careers in labor unions and became members of the United Automobile Workers of America International Union—the UAW. The UAW was a union of people who worked in factories around the United States making cars, trucks, and parts. It became the largest and most important union in the American automobile manufacturing industry. By the 1940s, the brothers were important leaders in the UAW.

All three brothers worked together, contributed to the labor movement, and earned international reputations as labor leaders. Walter Reuther became president of the UAW and one of the most important labor union leaders in the history of the United States. This is the story of Walter, Vic, and Roy—the Reuther brothers.

❖ 2 ❖

Anna and Valentine

The story of the Reuther brothers begins in Germany in the 1800s. That is where their parents, Valentine and Anna, were born.

Valentine Reuther was born in 1881 in the village of Edigheim, in an area in Germany known as the Rhineland. His father and mother, Jacob and Christina, were peasants—poor farmers who owned very small plots of land. Like millions of Germans, Italians, Poles, Greeks, Russians, and people from other foreign lands who hoped to make a new and better life for themselves during this era, the family immigrated to the United States in 1892 when Valentine was eleven years old.

Jacob and Christina settled their family on a small dairy farm in Effingham, Illinois. As a child, Valentine helped his father and mother on the family farm. There was much to be done: milking and feeding cows, chopping wood, and plenty of other chores.

The life of a farmer, however, was not the life for Valentine Reuther. When he was eighteen years old, Valentine decided it was time to leave and try to find a job in the city. In the fall of 1899, he helped his father harvest the crops one last time and then moved to Wheeling, West Virginia. His brother Jake had already moved to Wheeling and he helped Valentine find a job in a factory that made iron products and a room at a boarding house, which provided him with a bed and meals. At the iron-works, Valentine worked for twelve hours each day, six days a week, and made $1.50 per day. Valentine joined the union at

Christina and Jacob Reuther, the parents of Valentine Reuther, holding an unidentified child, probably on their farm near Effingham,
Illinois, in the early 1920s.

Anna and Valentine Reuther's wedding portrait, 1904.

the factory, the Amalgamated Association of Iron, Steel, and Tin Workers.

In 1904, Valentine took a job as a delivery wagon driver for the Schmulbach Brewing Company in Wheeling. Each day, he delivered beer around the city in a horse-drawn beer wagon through sun, snow, and rain and took care of his team of horses, brushing and feeding them. It was hard work, but a steady job.

Valentine joined the local branch of the International Union of Brewery Workers and soon became active in the union, giving speeches, and encouraging others to join. Although he still had a heavy German accent when he spoke English, Valentine gained a reputation as a skilled speaker and a strong supporter of unions. Over the years, he spoke at local union meetings and at the Wheeling city hall. Valentine even gave a speech in Charleston, the capital of West Virginia. Through his speeches, he tried to encourage workers to join unions or to vote for particular candidates in elections for all kinds of government positions, from city mayor to president of the United States.

In 1904, Valentine married Anna Stocker. When Valentine met the red-haired Anna, she was twenty-two years old and worked in the kitchen of a local tavern. Anna had immigrated by herself to the United States from her home in Scharnhausen, Germany, only twenty months earlier.

Anna had a very independent spirit. When she was seventeen, she began to talk about marrying her boyfriend, Fritz. Her mother, who was also a very strong-willed woman, would not hear of such things. She did not want her daughter to marry someone whose family had no property.

In desperation, Anna declared: "If you won't let me marry Fritz, then I'll go to America!" Her mother replied: "All right. I'd rather have you go to America than marry Fritz!" Anna would not back down from her threat to leave home. In 1902, she immigrated to America and joined her brother in Wheeling, West Virginia. Fritz stayed in Germany.

Eventually, Valentine and Anna married and moved into a house on Wetzel Street in south Wheeling. They had five chil-

dren: Theodore "Ted," in 1905, Walter Philip in 1907, Roy
Louis in 1909, Victor George in 1912, and Christina, the only
girl, in 1922.

❖ 3 ❖
Life in Wheeling

The Reuther brothers grew up in Wheeling, West Virginia, during the 1910s and 1920s. Wheeling was an industrial town with many factories that employed thousands of people to make iron, steel, and glass. Like many industrial towns in America, a large portion of its factory workers were immigrants from Germany, Poland, Sweden, Ireland, and other foreign lands, as well as from other parts of America. The Reuther brothers were like many other children who lived in their neighborhood on Wetzel Street. Their parents were also immigrants.

As parents, Anna and Valentine were a great influence upon their children, teaching them to work hard, spend money wisely, and do their best to help other people. The brothers learned about their German heritage from their parents, its traditions and culture. Most of all they were taught the importance of learning new skills and the value of an education.

From their mother, the brothers learned about religion and family life. She insisted that her children attend services every Sunday at the local Lutheran Church, and she worked very hard to manage the Reuther family household, especially during times when Valentine was unable to work. When the family had little money, Anna taught the brothers to be frugal, to make every dollar last as long as possible.

From their father, the brothers learned about politics and unions. Throughout his life, Valentine was always interested in the political affairs of Wheeling, the United States, and the world. But he devoted most of his energy and talents to the labor union of which he was a member. Valentine believed that every working person should join a labor union.

In the early 1900s, when America became one of the world's most powerful industrial nations, its factories, mines, and other industries needed millions of people to operate them. Many of these workers were immigrants from other countries. And many of them worked for low wages, without health insurance or other benefits, in jobs that were often dangerous. "People who work under these conditions," Valentine would tell his sons, "should join together and become members of a union." Then the union could bargain with business owners for better wages and working conditions for its members. Later in life, Walter said: "At my father's knee, we learned the philosophy [the ideas] of trade unionism . . . we got [learned about] the struggles, the hopes and aspirations of working people every day." The Reuther brothers never forgot these lessons.

Valentine also valued education. He believed that self improvement was a virtue and constantly worked to improve his knowledge of English, American history, and the political issues of the day. During after-dinner debates on Sunday afternoons—in fact, on any day of the week—Valentine would teach Ted, Walter, Roy, and Victor his ideas on trade unions and politics. Most important, he told his children that there was more to life than making money. "Success in life should not be measured in terms of fortunes made," Valentine would say, "but rather in service rendered, in good deeds done, in friends made."

The Reuther family knew how it felt to have little money for food and clothes. There were families in Wheeling that were poorer—the Reuthers did always manage to survive the tough times—but this experience left a life-long impression upon the brothers.

The worst times came in 1914 when, after working ten years for the Schmulbach Brewery, Valentine lost his job as a driver. In 1912, the legislature in West Virginia passed a law

Walter and Ted Reuther about 1909.

that prohibited the sale and production of alcoholic beverages in the state. When the law went into effect in 1914, the sale of beer became illegal, and the Schmulbach Brewery Company closed its doors forever. All its employees, including Valentine, were out of work.

For the next few years, the family had little money. Because Valentine was not a skilled worker such as a carpenter or an electrician, it was hard to find a job. He regretted his lack of skills and his poor education and because of this, Valentine urged his sons more than ever to become skilled workers, to learn a trade.

Valentine attempted to operate a restaurant, but this venture soon ended when he was injured. One day, while moving cartons of warm soda pop into his restaurant, one of the bottles exploded and a small piece of sharp glass flew into Valentine's eye. He could not work for a long time and he never regained the sight in that eye. For the next few years, Valentine was unable to find a steady full-time job that would support his family of six.

Anna did everything she could to get the most from each dollar the family spent. Empty flour sacks were made into underwear, and she made her own soap. Like many families during this era, to earn extra money the Reuthers rented rooms in their house to working men who did not have their own apartments or homes. Anna cooked hundreds of meals for these boarders, all while attending to her own family. The brothers were expected to pitch in and help their mother take care of the boarders. They carried water, chopped wood—their home had no running water or electricity—and helped Anna clean and prepare meals. Every member cared for and supported the other.

The Reuther family's situation had improved greatly by the time the last child, Christina, was born in 1922. A few years after losing his eye, Valentine took a job as a life insurance salesman. He soon built a growing business and, by the 1920s, the family had a modest but steady income.

❖ 4 ❖
Making Choices

It was tough growing up during the years when their father was out of work, and the experience shaped the lives of the Reuther brothers forever. Walter, Roy, and Victor became very close pals and remained so throughout their lives. Eventually, as adults, they would work together as members of the United Automobile Workers union. But, as teenagers, each of the brothers seemed to take a different path.

The oldest brother, Ted, had to go to work at an early age. In 1916, when he was eleven years old, Ted began to take part-time jobs to earn some badly needed cash for the family. After he finished the eighth grade in school, he completed a course in bookkeeping at a local business school and began a full-time job.

Thereafter, Ted's life became much different from that of his younger brothers. Ted worked very hard and had little time to play with them. In the 1930s, Walter, Roy, and Victor moved away from Wheeling and worked together in Detroit, Michigan. Ted worked, married, raised a family, and lived in Wheeling for the rest of his life.

When the family moved to a farm on Bethlehem Hill, on the north side of Wheeling in 1926, Ted was working at the Wheeling Corrugating Company. The company's factory specialized in making long, thin sheets of steel that could be shaped into other products. He worked in the office at the Wheeling Corrugating factory as a bookkeeper for forty-eight years.

CHAPTER 4

The Reuther family about 1918.

The tool and die shop at Wheeling Corrugated Company in Wheeling, West Virginia, about 1927. Walter is at the upper right.

One of Ted's first jobs was in the Northwood Glass Factory, where children were hired to work "half-shifts," or five hours a day. Ted often worked two half-shifts to earn eighty cents to add to the family income.

Walter loved watching Ted at work making glass and would often visit him at the factory. There were no safety rules in 1916, and children would often wander through the glass factory. One day, Walter almost lost an eye. He was struck in the face by a long, iron blowpipe used to make glass. It had a bit of molten glass on the end that hit Walter on the side of his nose. His eye and face healed, but he carried a scar on his nose for the rest of his life.

Left to right: Ted, Roy, Christine, Victor, and Walter outside their West Virginia home about 1928.

Walter had his mother's independent spirit, her courage, and her red hair. During the debates his father held on Sundays, he was a smart, fiery speaker and always tried to gather as much information as possible for his arguments. Walter had a natural aptitude for mechanical work and would visit local machine shops and factories in his spare time, watching the workers and learning about their trades.

Walter was the daredevil brother that decided to jump off a neighborhood water tower with an umbrella. At a fair, he had watched a man parachute from an airplane. Fascinated, he decided to try parachuting himself. His experiment did not work. The umbrella folded under his weight, and he crashed to the ground. Luckily, he did not seriously injure himself; just a few bumps and bruises, and a lesson learned.

In 1923, when he was sixteen, Walter took a job at the Wheeling Corrugated Company. Ted told him that there was a job opening as an apprentice in the factory's tool room. Walter immediately dropped out of school and took the job. He worked there for the next three years, learning the skills of a die maker, a tradesperson who knew how to shape hardened steel into dies or forms. The forms were then used in metal-shaping machines to turn raw metal into parts for such products as automobile engines and kitchen stoves. Because of their skills, die makers were the most respected of all the tradespeople who worked with metal.

Like his older brothers, Roy was a good student. He was also a very good basketball player at school. At the family's Sunday debates, Roy spoke softly and smoothly, carefully choosing his words. Roy's real passion as a teenager, however, was electrical work. He wired the family's barn and built a radio set from a kit so that the family could listen to broadcasts from radio stations in nearby Pittsburgh, Pennsylvania.

The family was doing well with both Ted and Walter at work, and Roy did not have to hold a part-time job while he attended school. Still, he decided to take an apprenticeship as an electrician at a nearby electrical factory, dropping out of high school before he finished his degree. Like his father, Roy joined the local union at the electrical company and was soon involved in union activities.

Victor, who loved to read and was the most emotional speaker at Sunday debates, was the only brother to finish high school. As the youngest brother, by the time he entered high school, the family income had grown to the point where Victor did not have to work. He was the most bookish of the brothers: he had a passion for history and literature, and spent hours reading books at the local library, learning about the ideas of great writers and political leaders. Victor was also a fine speaker and was president of his high school debating club. In 1929, Victor enrolled at the University of West Virginia and began to take classes. At this point in his life, he decided he would like to become a lawyer. Walter and Roy sent money to Victor, allowing him to pay for his college classes.

Walter, Roy, and Victor remained very close during their growing-up years. They played sports together, camped together, and worked together. When Walter and Roy took full-

Left to right: Walter, Roy, Victor, and Ted on a visit to the Virginia seashore in 1927.

time jobs, the brothers spent less time together, but they still lived at home with Anna, Valentine, Ted, and their little sister, Christina. These were also years of learning as each brother worked hard to improve his skills, whether debating with their father, reading a book, working to make a tool, or building electrical systems for a machine.

The first break in the family occurred in 1927. For three years, Walter had developed his skills while working in the machine shop at the Wheeling Corrugated factory and was now a very good die maker. Walter was making a good rate of pay in Wheeling—forty-two cents an hour—but he had heard a great deal about high-paying jobs in the automobile business in a city in Michigan. The family was doing well and no longer needed the money he earned. On February 27, 1927, nineteen-year-old Walter moved to Detroit.

❖ 5 ❖
Going to Detroit

In 1927, when Walter moved to Detroit, it was one of the best places in the world to find a good paying job. Around the world, Detroit was known as the Motor City. The city earned this name because, since 1914, Detroit had produced more cars than any place on earth. The automobile industry needed workers like Walter, skilled people who could shape metal into tools and parts.

Detroit was America's fourth largest city, with a population of over one and a half million people. The manufacturing of cars and trucks was the largest industry in Detroit as well as in the state of Michigan. Every day, thousands of cars were made in Detroit—Fords, Dodges, Cadillacs, Chryslers, and others. Throughout the city, hundreds of factories assembled finished cars, while other factories made parts for cars or turned iron ore into steel. Hundreds of thousands of skilled and unskilled workers were needed to make the cars.

Walter traveled with his friend, Leo Hores, to Detroit. Leo was six years older than Walter and a skilled die maker. They arrived on a Saturday and stayed with friends of Valentine. The next day, Walter and Leo found rooms at a boarding house. Much like Anna did in Wheeling, many people in Detroit earned extra money by providing beds and meals to working men and women. Walter could only pay for a few nights at the boarding house; he had to find a job on Monday.

By Monday afternoon, Walter was employed as a drill press operator for the Briggs Manufacturing Company. He was paid sixty cents an hour to operate the large drill used to bore through hardened metal. The Briggs Company's factory made metal car bodies and sold them to automobile makers that assembled and sold the finished cars. The company was successful, but it was a dangerous place to work. Many workers were injured—most suffered cuts and bruises, some lost fingers or hands in the machinery, and a few workers died in accidents. Because there were so many accidents at the Briggs factory, in Detroit it became known as "the slaughterhouse."

After three weeks in the Briggs factory, Walter decided he would find a better place to work. He heard that the Ford Motor Company, which was owned by Henry Ford, was hiring tool and die makers. Since 1908, the Ford Motor Company had made and sold over 15 million Ford Model T's, the most famous car in the world. In 1927, however, the company planned to replace the Model T with a new car, the Model A. To be able to make the new car, Ford's factories had to be retooled—machines that assembled the Model T now had to assemble the Model A. New tools and dies were needed to shape metal into parts for the new car. To retool its factories, Ford needed a great number of highly skilled tool and die makers.

Walter went to the Ford factory in Highland Park, which was then a nearby suburb of Detroit, and announced that he would like to apply for a job as a die maker. At first, the guard at the factory door said: "Get on your way, you're just a kid." But Walter would not leave until he was given an interview. On this day and throughout his life, Walter was persistent: he never quit trying to accomplish the goals he set for himself. Finally, after three hours of arguing with Walter, the guard let him speak to George Gardham, the manager who hired tool and die makers.

Mr. Gardham thought Walter was young for the job, too, but he was impressed with Walter's determination to succeed. After Walter showed his skill at reading blueprints, or plans for new dies, Gardham said: "I'll make you a deal. . . . if you are willing to go to work without knowing what you are going to get paid for two days, we will watch you carefully and at the

Ford Model A assembly line, 1930.

end of two days we'll decide whether we are going to keep you and what we are willing to pay you." Walter agreed to the deal. After two days of work, Gardham said: "You've surprised all of us and you can stay. Your rate will be $1.05 per hour." Walter worked for the Ford Motor Company for the next five years.

Walter was advancing his skills as a die maker, but he was painfully aware that his education was still incomplete. After he was transferred to Ford Motor Company's huge River Rouge factory complex in Dearborn, Michigan, Walter enrolled at Dearborn's Fordson High School. Although he had a promising career as a die maker, Walter never forgot his father's lessons about the value of education. On his application for a

Walter and his roommates in Detroit, 1930. *Left to right:* Reuther, Ralph Churchill, Louis Gardner, and Alec Walker.

Left to right: Walter, Victor, and Ted on a camping trip in 1926.

Victor, Roy, and Walter standing on a mountain during their trip to Virginia in 1926.

school club he wrote: "I realize that to do something constructive in life, one must have an education. I seek knowledge that I may serve mankind."

For the next two years, every day was extremely busy for Walter: he had to study in the early morning, rush to his classes at Fordson, and afterwards ride a bus to the Ford factory where he made dies from 4:00 P.M. until midnight. Walter was a dedicated student, and in 1929 he earned his high school diploma.

By that time, Walter had also become a die leader for the Ford Motor Company, a person who led a group of fifteen to twenty die makers in the factory, and he was making $1.40 an hour. This was very good pay and made him one of the highest paid factory workers. At that time, most unskilled people who worked on automobile assembly lines made four dollars a week. Walter's high rate of pay even allowed him to save some money for the future.

In the spring of 1929, the Reuther brothers reunited for a vacation. Traveling in Ted's Model T Ford, they visited many sites in Washington, D.C., and Richmond, Virginia, and camped in the nearby Blue Ridge Mountains. It was a wonderful time and the brothers strengthened the bonds between themselves.

A few weeks earlier, Walter had asked Victor: "Why don't you come to Detroit and we'll work and study together?" Victor decided that Walter's idea was a good one and he moved to Detroit.

❖ 6 ❖

The Depression

Victor journeyed to the Motor City in the fall of 1930. Upon arrival, he moved into a basement apartment with Walter and three of his friends near the College of the City of Detroit—which later became Wayne State University. The city, however, had changed since Walter moved there three years earlier. In 1930, Detroit was feeling the effects of the Great Depression and jobs were almost impossible to find.

The Great Depression was a world-wide economic crisis which began in the fall of 1929 and lasted for most of the 1930s. It was the worst economic time in American history. In October 1929, the American stock market, where people bought and sold shares of various companies, suddenly collapsed. This stock market "crash" caused tremendous financial loss for thousands of businesses in the United States. Within two years, five thousand banks went out of business and over thirty-two thousand businesses, from small stores to huge companies, closed their doors forever. Millions of people lost their jobs and there was widespread poverty in America.

During 1932, the worst year of the Depression, twelve million people were out of work. Almost 25 percent, or one of every four working Americans, lost their jobs. That same year in Detroit, nearly half of the city's workforce was without a job.

When Victor arrived in Detroit, automobile companies were laying off workers, telling them that they no longer had jobs. Money was scarce during the Depression, and Americans were not buying expensive items such as automobiles. This meant that Detroit's factories built fewer cars and, therefore, needed fewer people to design, make, and sell cars. Victor had little hope of finding a job.

Luckily, Walter was still employed at Ford and still earning very good wages. He had become such a good die maker that he was in charge of forty other die makers. And Walter was frugal: he had even saved enough money to buy a bit of land and pay for college classes.

Victor told Walter: "I could not have picked a worse time to come to Detroit." He was worried about having no job and no money.

"Victor, I know there are no jobs in Detroit," said Walter, "but this is what we will do. There are five of us living in this apartment now, and the four of us who still have jobs at Ford have little time to cook meals and clean. To help all of us, why don't you cook our meals and help us take care of our apartment? This will benefit all of us. And, I will give you sixty dollars to pay for classes at the College of the City of Detroit. We can take classes together and help each other with homework and study for exams!" Victor accepted the offer, and the brothers enrolled at college.

On Walter's application to the College of the City of Detroit there was a statement from his high school principle, Forrest G. Averill. "In my opinion," Mr. Averill said, Walter was "one of the best boys we have ever graduated. *He will Succeed.*"

For Walter and Victor, it was like old times in Wheeling. The brothers spent little time apart from each other and became closer than ever. They attended classes together, studied together, and explored the city together.

For three years, Walter had concentrated on his work and his education, but Victor's arrival in Detroit renewed his interest in politics. Walter was full of questions and ideas, and a born leader who could influence others. Victor's constant interest in books and ideas, along with his fine speaking skills, certainly helped shape Walter's opinions. Merlin Bishop, who lived with the brothers, said: "Their minds were like one."

The greatest influence upon the brothers during these years was the Great Depression. Every day they saw the dev-

A homeless man in the entrance to his dugout home in Detroit about 1930. Photograph by Victor or Walter.

astating poverty the Depression had brought to Detroit. From the front window of the apartment they shared with their friends, Walter and Victor saw people walking with nothing but rags on their feet, searching garbage cans for something to eat.

To learn more about the problems the Depression caused, Walter and Victor explored Detroit, observing and taking pictures of a city in a crisis. They saw thousands of men without jobs walking the streets, hoping to find even one day's work for pay. Many families in Detroit lost their homes when they could not pay their house payments, and the brothers found

Long underwear belonging to an unemployed homeless man in Detroit, drying on a fence near his dugout home about 1930. Photograph by Victor or Walter.

Young boys outside a store in Detroit during the Great Depression, about 1930. Photograph by Victor or Walter.

them living in shacks made of whatever materials they could find on city streets and in garbage dumps. Areas in the city where homeless men, women, and children lived in shacks or tents were named "Hoovervilles" after Herbert C. Hoover, who was president of the United States when the Great Depression hit the nation in 1929. To try to understand how it felt to have no place to live, Walter and Victor dressed up as homeless people and spent a weekend in a Salvation Army shelter for homeless men.

The Reuther brothers were deeply moved by what they saw and decided that they must do something. At the College of the City of Detroit, along with friends such as Merlin Bishop, Walter and Victor formed the Social Problems Club. At the club's meetings, students gathered to discuss the problems of the city and the nation. Walter and Victor made public speeches, discussing the needs of the poor, demanding equal job opportunities for all Americans, and encouraging workers to join labor unions.

Roy joined Walter and Victor in Detroit in the summer of 1932. He had been laid off from his job in Wheeling and, with little prospect of finding work in that city, decided to join his brothers in the Motor City. Walter and Victor had recently moved with two friends to a larger apartment on Merrick Street, and there was plenty of room for Roy. Like his brothers, Roy enrolled in college classes at the College of the City of Detroit and joined the Social Problems Club.

With Roy now living in Detroit, the Reuther brothers became more involved in labor unions. In particular, they became interested in working conditions in Detroit's automobile factories.

During the Depression, work in automobile factories was tough. There were few safety devices on machinery, and autoworkers had to work hard and fast to keep up with the speed of the moving assembly line. There were no unions, and those who could not work fast enough or complained about working conditions lost their jobs. One union leader described the way autoworkers were treated during this time: "There was no dignity."

Walter began to discuss politics with his fellow workers at Ford and, along with Victor and Roy, he joined the tiny Auto Workers Union, which had only a few members. It was hard to get people to join labor unions during the Depression. Jobs were scarce, and the automobile companies did not want unions in their factories or influencing their businesses. Foremen in the factories, the men who were responsible for hiring and managing workers, would often fire those who spoke in favor of unions.

In November 1932, Walter lost his job at Ford. Although his foreman never explained why he was laid off, Walter assumed that his discussions of politics and unions with fellow workers at Ford led to his downfall.

Walter, who was always a self-confident, determined young man, did not brood over losing his job. He told Victor: "I've been fired. Now I'm free and nothing stands in our way. We can go on that trip."

❖ 7 ❖

The Big Adventure

For a long time, Walter and Victor had dreamed of a trip around the world. They wanted to visit many places and see how other people around the world lived and worked. There were relatives in Germany to visit, and the brothers wanted to see the towns where Valentine and Anna were born. They also hoped to travel to England, France, and other countries. It would be a big adventure, Walter and Victor thought, and a great opportunity to study working people and unions in other lands. Walter stated: "We planned this world tour to get a practical background for our future work."

Walter had saved enough money to pay for a few months in Europe—if they watched their spending. To make their adventure a long one, however, the brothers would have to find jobs in another country to pay for their travels.

Before Walter lost his job, he learned about an automobile factory in Russia—then a part of the nation called the Soviet Union—that needed die makers and other skilled workers. Ford Motor Company had sold the machines, tools, and dies needed to make Model A Ford cars to the Soviet Union. In a city called Gorky, a factory was being built that would use the equipment from Ford to make cars in Russia. At this time, the Soviet Union had few skilled workers; most of the Russians who worked in the factory were peasant farmers without training in industrial skills. Ford had sent technicians to Gorky to help install the machinery in the factory, and Russian workers had traveled to Detroit to learn about machines, tools, and dies, but more skilled workers were needed to operate the fac-

45

tory. The Soviet government was looking for skilled workers to go to Gorky and teach the Russian peasants how to build cars.

Encouraged by a friend who was already working at the factory, Walter signed up to go to Gorky. Walter insisted that Victor be allowed to go as well. Victor had never worked in a factory and had no industrial skills, but this did not bother Walter, who decided he could teach Victor the basic skills of a tool and die maker.

Before they left for Europe, Walter and Victor visited their family home in Wheeling for a few weeks. In the evenings, Walter and Victor spent their time in the machine shop at Wheeling High School, where their former teacher, Mr. Schneider, allowed them to work. Within a few weeks, Walter taught Victor the basic skills he would need to be an instructor for the Russian peasants.

Valentine and Anna thought the trip was a good idea. Their sons would be able to visit relatives in Germany that their parents had not seen for years, and they would learn a great deal about the world. But Valentine and Anna were also a little bit worried. Walter and Victor would be so far from home, and the brothers did not know how long they would be away from their parents.

A farewell party for the two Reuther brothers was held at their family home. The local Wheeling newspaper wrote a small story about the party and included a quote by Walter that explained why the brothers were going on their trip: "We are going to study the economic and social conditions of the world, not the bright lights."

The brothers returned to Detroit to prepare for their adventure. Walter withdrew the money he had saved and bought warm coats and boots for himself and Victor. The brothers also bought two sets of die maker's tools, which they would carry with them to Gorky. They said good-bye to Roy, who was staying in Detroit, where he was working with the Auto Workers Union.

Since he moved to Detroit, Roy had worked as an organizer for labor unions. As an organizer, he worked to enroll factory workers as members of unions and gave speeches about the advantages of joining a labor union. That summer, Roy was going to take classes at the Brookwood Labor College in New York, a school that taught its students about organizing and building labor unions. It was an opportunity he did not want to miss. Roy stayed at Brookwood as a student and later as a teacher for most of the time Walter and Victor were away.

On the evening of February 16, 1933, Walter and Victor boarded the German ocean liner *SS Deutschland* in New York City and sailed for the port of Hamburg, Germany. They would not return to the United States for almost three years.

❖ 8 ❖

Exploring Europe

After an ocean voyage of eight days, Walter and Victor arrived in Hamburg, Germany. The brothers then made their way to Berlin, the largest city in Germany, where they went to the local office of the Amtorg Trading Company. Amtorg, owned by the government of the Soviet Union, was the company that recruited Walter and Victor to work in the Gorky automobile factory. They asked about their tickets and passes to Russia—both brothers had learned to speak the German language as children from their parents—but they learned that it would be several months before they could travel to Russia.

The brothers had expected a small delay in their travel to Russia. Nine months passed, however, before there was a place for them to stay in Gorky. Walter and Victor were concerned: they would have to make their money last as long as possible. But there was a good side to the problem. The brothers had more time to spend with their relatives and to travel around Europe.

First, Walter and Victor visited their relatives who lived in the state of Swabia in southwest Germany. The brothers took a train to Ruit, a small village near Stuttgart where Uncle Ernst, Aunt Karolina, and their cousins, Erna and Julia, lived. When they got off the train, they found a small handcart Uncle Ernst had left for them at the station. Walter and Victor loaded their clothes and tool boxes on the cart and walked two miles

Walter and Victor with German relatives in Ruit, Germany, 1933.

to their uncle's house, where they received a warm welcome.

The trip from Hamburg to Ruit, however, had been a disturbing experience. The brothers had arrived in Germany at the same time that Adolf Hitler and his Nazi political party were gaining power. Everywhere they traveled in Germany, Walter and Victor saw the flag of the Nazi Party and Hitler's followers, called "storm troopers," dressed in brown-shirted uniforms. While the brothers were in Germany in 1933, Hitler was taking a brutal path to power. Hitler was an extreme racist, fixing his hatred upon whole groups of people such as Africans and Jews. He made speeches full of hate toward anyone who disagreed. His storm troopers beat up, arrested, or, in some cases, killed anyone who protested Hitler's actions. By the end of the year, Hitler had outlawed trade unions and all political parties except the Nazi Party and was in control of all state governments in Germany. One year later, Hitler was the dictator of Germany, in complete control of that nation.

The rise of the Nazis and their brutal ways left a deep and lasting impression upon the Reuther brothers. They saw firsthand what happened to a nation when its people lost their freedom of speech and their right to vote in a democratic government.

Victor and Walter on bicycles during their tour of Europe, 1934.

The rise of the Nazi Party even affected the brothers' family in Germany. Uncle Ernst believed in a democratic government and was a member of a labor union. Uncle Adolph, who owned a small farm near Ruit, was a follower of Hitler. The uncles often argued, sometimes screaming at each other.

Walter and Victor decided to use the extra time before they went to Gorky for travel in Europe. They bought two bicycles and added metal containers to each to hold their clothes and travel gear. Using Ruit as their home base, the place to which they would return after each trip, the brothers bicycled over six thousand miles through other European nations such as Austria, England, France, and Italy. It was a great time for them.

In both England and France, Walter and Victor visited automobile factories to talk with other workers and attend meetings of labor unions. There were strong labor unions in many European nations. The brothers met important union leaders and made many friends. It was an exciting time, to say the least, that provided Walter and Victor with knowledge and experience they would use when they returned to Detroit.

The brothers had only one serious mishap while biking through Europe. One day, in England, they decided to make their pedaling easier by holding onto the back of a moving truck. When the truck took a sudden turn, Walter and Victor went flying onto the street. Walter's right arm was badly twisted and cut. After a doctor sewed the cut in his arm together with six stitches, the always determined Walter asked Victor to help him onto his bike, and they rode off. It would be several weeks, however, before Walter's arm was healed.

When the brothers returned to Germany, their train tickets and the official passes they needed to travel to the Soviet Union were waiting for them. In November 1933, Walter and Victor boarded a train that would take them to Gorky.

❖ 9 ❖

Working in Gorky

When Walter and Victor arrived in Gorky, the temperature was thirty-five degrees below zero. They were dressed in light clothes and thin socks and were nearly frozen when they finally made their way to the "American Village."

The American Village was the place where skilled workers from the United States, Finland, England, Germany, Austria, Italy, and other countries lived. The village consisted of two crude wooden buildings near the Gorky automobile factory. The buildings were cold and there were no kitchens. Only cold water came from taps located in the hallway, and everyone who lived in the buildings shared the bathrooms. The meals provided for the foreign workers were poor, usually a chunk of heavy black bread and a bowl of cabbage soup. Meat and vegetables were rare.

Walter and Victor soon found that the automobile factory was as poorly built as their living quarters. The only heat in the whole factory was in the heat treat department, which had a furnace for heating steel to temper it or make it stronger. Like the Russian workers, the brothers soon wore thick felt boots on their feet, fur caps on their heads, and heavy coats under their shop aprons while in the factory. During the coldest months of the Russian winter, Walter and Victor could only work for thirty minutes before they had to warm their hands in the heat treat department.

Still, the Reuther brothers enjoyed their adventure at Gorky. They especially liked working with the Russian workers

Apartments for workers at the Gorky automobile factory in the Soviet Union, 1935.

in the factory. Walter and Victor learned to speak the Russian language, which allowed them to talk with their coworkers and learn about their customs and history. Lunch breaks in the factory, when the Russians would play music and dance, were especially interesting for the brothers.

Walter and Victor thought they were doing a good deed, teaching industrial skills in a nation that was desperate for technological knowledge. Walter often wrote letters to the newspapers in Moscow, the largest city in the Soviet Union, praising the spirit of the Russian peasants as they struggled to change themselves from farmers into factory workers. He also wrote letters suggesting improvements as well as complaining about the lack of materials, safety devices, and tools.

But there was a dark side to their adventure in Gorky.

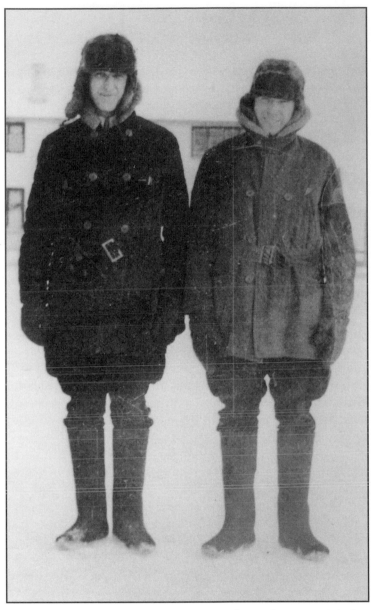

Victor and Walter on their way to work at the Gorky automobile factory, 1934.

Much like Germany, the Soviet Union was a troubled nation.

The Soviet Union was born out of a bloody revolution. In 1917, Russia was a nation ruled by one man, the Czar or king, who descended from a royal family that had ruled Russia since 1689. The Czar was wealthy and had a large army, but most people in Russia lived as peasant farmers, barely making a living. There was a revolution in 1917, followed by a civil war, and when the fighting stopped, the communists had won. Russia was reformed as the Soviet Union with the Communist Party in control of the government.

Communists believed the national government should own all of a nation's land, businesses, and trade and manage them for the benefit of all its citizens. There would be no private property and the Communist Party would control the government and work to improve the life of all of its citizens. A noble idea, perhaps, but one that did not work in the Soviet Union.

By the time the Reuther brothers were in Gorky, a man named Joseph Stalin had risen to power in the Soviet Union. Like Hitler, he soon became a dictator. Indeed, in 1934, while Walter and Victor were working in Gorky, Stalin began a series of "purges," getting rid of anyone who opposed him. Within a few years, he arrested millions of Russians, sending most to prison, and executing many others including rival Communist Party members, teachers, professors, writers, peasants, and generals. With Stalin exercising almost unlimited control of the Soviet Union, freedom of speech and other basic freedoms were eliminated.

The Reuther brothers were not directly affected by Stalin's actions. Because the Soviet Union desperately needed skilled workers, Gorky generally remained safe for Walter, Victor, and most of the other foreign skilled workers in Gorky, but the situation for Russian workers was rapidly changing. They would no longer speak freely with the brothers. Worse than that, several people Walter and Victor worked with in Gorky suddenly disappeared and were never seen again.

By the spring of 1935, most of the foreign workers had already left Gorky. The Reuther brothers had been paid very

A worker showing others how to operate a press in the Gorky automobile factory in the Soviet Union about 1934.

well over the last year and had saved some money. They left Gorky and finished their adventure by first traveling to tourist sites in the Soviet Union, then taking a train across China to its eastern border. Once there, Walter and Victor took a boat to Japan, where they bought bicycles to replace the ones they had left behind. They pedaled through Japan, seeing the sights, until their money was gone.

Luckily for the brothers, they found work on the S.S. *Hoover*, an American ocean liner about to set sail for the United States. Walter worked below deck, cleaning and wiping the ship's engines, while Victor cleaned the ship's decks and polished its brass rails and trim. In the fall of 1935, after nearly three years away from home, Walter and Victor landed in Los Angeles, California. They went directly to Wheeling for a reunion with their family.

Walter, who was now twenty-eight years old, and Victor, age twenty-three, returned to the United States as men of the world. They had traveled through many lands, observing people living and working, and they had made many friends. Walter and Victor also witnessed the rise of two terrible dictators in Germany and the Soviet Union. All of their experiences added to their education and convinced them that the way to improve the life of working people in the United States was through labor unions.

Detroit was a fine place for Walter, Roy, and Victor to begin their careers as labor union leaders. Already known around the world as the Motor City, in the 1930s Detroit earned a reputation as the leading labor union city in America. Many of the most important events in the history of the labor movement occurred in Detroit. The Reuther brothers would soon make their mark upon this history.

❖ 10 ❖

Building the UAW

In 1936, a few months after Walter and Victor returned to America, the Reuther brothers were reunited in Detroit. That same year, Walter, Victor, and Roy began their careers with the United Automobile Workers union, the UAW. They would work for the UAW for the rest of their lives.

Detroit and the United States had changed during the years Walter and Victor were away. Detroit was leading the way in the nation's new labor movement. America also had a new president, Franklin D. Roosevelt, who supported unions and had once said: "If I worked in a factory, I would join a union." When he became president in 1933, Roosevelt and his supporters passed new laws to try to raise the United States out of the Great Depression. One of the new laws made it easier to organize labor unions and, by 1936, many unions had been formed in various industries.

One of the new unions was the UAW. It was formed in 1935 to organize skilled and unskilled workers in automobile factories throughout the United States. First, local UAW unions were organized at each factory or at a group of factories. Then, the local unions joined together to form the international UAW, which was, and still is, led by an elected president. The UAW was formed as a democratic union: all of its leaders are elected by the votes of UAW members.

When the Reuther brothers joined the UAW in 1936, it was a small union of a few thousand members, but it was growing rapidly. There were over 300,000 autoworkers in Detroit, and

Children picketing the Dodge Main factory in Hamtramck, Michigan, during the 1948 Chrysler strike.

in many factories they were treated poorly. They labored hard and fast in unsafe conditions for low pay, and could not question any company decision that affected their work for fear of losing their jobs. Under these conditions, more and more autoworkers decided to join the UAW.

Automobile companies did everything they could to keep the UAW out of their factories. They did not want unions to have any influence on their business decisions and fought every effort the UAW made to gain pay raises or other benefits for its members. The companies hired people to pose as factory workers and spy on other autoworkers, trying to find union

Walter *(standing)* at a UAW strategy meeting during a strike at General Motors, 1939. Victor is sitting on the left.

organizers, who would then lose their jobs. Most of all, the auto companies refused to recognize the UAW as the official voice of the autoworkers.

Unions had only one real weapon to use to make the car companies listen—the strike. A strike occurred when all or most of the workers in a factory refused to work until the company agreed to bargain with them over pay raises or other work issues. The striking workers would then form lines outside the factory called "picket lines," to protest against the company's actions and block others from taking their jobs.

The Reuther brothers became some of the most active members of the UAW, quickly proving they did not lack

Roy, Victor, and Walter in Milwaukee during the 1937 UAW convention.

Genora Johnson, leader of the UAW Women's Emergency Brigade, helping her son, Jarvis, hold a picket sign during the sit-down strike against General Motors in Flint, Michigan, 1937.

energy and courage. In the fall of 1936, Walter and Victor led a successful strike at Kelsey-Hayes, a company that made parts for automobile brakes, winning wage increases for all of the company's workers and equal pay for men and women. In December 1936, Victor and Roy were leaders of a UAW sit-down strike at several General Motors factories in Flint, Michigan. It was called a sit-down strike because UAW members simply sat down in the factories and refused to work or to leave the building.

The Flint sit-down lasted for forty-four days. It ended when General Motors finally agreed to bargain with the UAW as the official representative of its autoworkers. It was the first big victory for the UAW.

Strikes were not pleasant. When autoworkers went on strike, they did not get paid for the days they were not working. If the strike lasted for a long time, it often meant that autoworkers' savings would run out and they could not pay their bills. And sometimes companies tried to hire replacement workers, which could result in fights between the striking workers and their replacements.

The Reuther brothers and other UAW organizers often faced danger when they attempted to encourage others to join the union. One day in May 1937, Walter and several other UAW members were peacefully giving pamphlets to Ford workers as they arrived for work at the huge River Rouge factory in Dearborn, Michigan, the largest factory in the world. Before the Depression, almost 100,000 people worked there every day.

Without warning, Ford security officers attacked the UAW members. According to government investigators, the UAW people were "knocked down and viciously pounded and kicked. . . . They were then raised in the air several times and thrown upon their backs on the concrete. [Walter] Reuther was then kicked down the north stairway and beaten and chased down Miller Road." A photographer from the *Detroit News*, the local daily newspaper, captured the beatings on film. Soon pictures of Walter Reuther and his friends, bruised and battered, were printed in newspapers and magazines around the United States. Walter earned a great deal of respect for his courage.

Walter delivering a speech in Detroit on Labor Day, 1961.

Throughout the UAW, the Reuther brothers earned reputations as courageous, intelligent union members. In particular, Walter soon became one of the leaders of the International UAW. In 1937, he was elected president of UAW Local 174, a local union of 30,000 members that Walter had organized on the west side of Detroit. Two years later, he was responsible for bargaining with the world's largest company, General Motors, and in 1942, he became a vice president of the international UAW. Within a few years, Walter had become one of the most respected labor union leaders in America.

❖ 11 ❖

Sweethearts and Families

The Reuther brothers worked closely together during the early years of the UAW, from 1936 to 1946. This was an important period of time in the public lives of the brothers. They did well in their chosen careers and helped build the UAW into a powerful union with over 500,000 members. This was also an important time in the personal lives of Walter, Victor, and Roy, when each of the brothers married their sweethearts.

Walter was married first. He met May Wolf, a physical education teacher at a Detroit city high school, shortly after returning to Detroit in the fall of 1935. They fell in love and were married in March 1936. May was an intelligent, outgoing woman, who was as strong-willed as Walter. She worked with the teachers union. Indeed, Walter and May were both so involved in the labor movement that they spent their wedding night at a rally for labor unions! For many years, May was Walter's personal secretary at the UAW Local 174, and throughout their lives they were partners in the labor movement. Walter and May raised two daughters: Linda and Elizabeth.

In July 1936, a few months after Walter and May were married, Victor married Sophie Goodlavich. It seemed that, even in matters of love, Walter and Victor followed in each other's footsteps. Victor met Sophie at the Brookwood Labor College in New York. Sophie was a neat polite young woman who, like Victor, was in love with books and ideas.

Walter and May Reuther about 1936.

Left to right: May, Walter, Roy, Sophie, Victor, and Fania Reuther about 1936. Seated on the ground is Christine Reuther.

A few months after Victor and Sophie met, Roy took a group of actors from Brookwood, which included Sophie, on a tour to perform a play in several cities. One of their stops was in Wheeling, West Virginia, at the home of Valentine and Anna. Victor was in love and decided he could wait no longer. He rushed from Detroit to the Reuther home and proposed to Sophie. Victor and Sophie eventually had three children: a daughter, Carole, and two sons, Eric and John.

Roy was the last Reuther brother to get married. Like Victor, Roy met his future wife, Fania Sasonkin, at Brookwood Labor College, where she was a student. Fania had been raised in a family like the Reuthers that believed in labor unions. Roy and Fania, married in 1944, had two sons: David and Alan.

It was tough to be married to one of the Reuther brothers, or to be their child. As leaders in the UAW, they spent many hours and many days away from their homes and families, attending union meetings, giving speeches, and walking in picket lines. The brothers loved their families, but they dedicated most of their time to the UAW, especially after 1946.

❖ 12 ❖

The Reuther Legacy

In 1946, Walter was elected president of the UAW, the highest position in the union. For the next twenty-four years, he would lead the UAW. Walter became the most famous brother, but Victor and Roy also held important positions in the UAW. Together, they helped make the UAW one of the most powerful unions in the world.

Once Walter was elected president by the members of the UAW, he was in a position to put his ideas to work. First and foremost, he and his brothers worked hard to bargain with automobile companies to improve the lives of UAW members. With Walter as president, the UAW grew to over 1.5 million members. This meant that the UAW represented the workers in thousands of factories around the United States and Canada and that it was strong enough to bargain for many improvements for its members.

In the 1940s, most automobile companies provided only a few benefits for their workers. During Walter Reuther's years as president, UAW members received increases in pay, as well as health care, vacations, safety regulations, pensions or savings for retirement, and other benefits, all as part of their pay for work. All of these improvements were the results of contracts between the various companies and the UAW.

Victor and Roy also held important positions in the UAW and contributed to its success while Walter was president. More importantly, the three brothers discussed ideas, planned new activities for the UAW, and supported each other in their work.

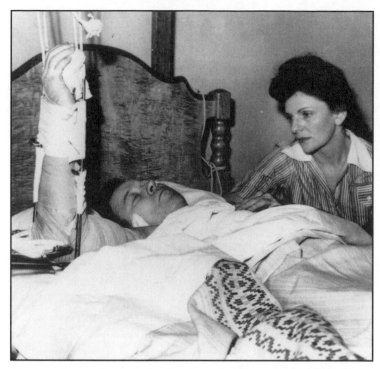

May Reuther at the bedside of Walter after the attempt on his life in 1948.

Even with the support of his brothers, Walter alone could not build the UAW. He had to have the support of UAW members. Although not all agreed with Walter's ideas and politics, the overwhelming majority of UAW members considered him to be the best labor leader in the world, and they continued to elect Walter as president until 1970.

It was hard work being leaders of the UAW. Most Americans did not belong to labor unions and believed that labor unions interfered with business decisions that should be left to company owners. Many times, the UAW found it necessary to call strikes to force companies to make contracts with its members. And no one, including the UAW, liked strikes.

Some Americans believed that all union members were communists. Since Walter and Victor had worked in the Soviet Union, they were often accused of being communists. The opposite was true. The Reuther brothers believed in democracy and worked to remove communists from the UAW.

Sometimes, being a union leader was very dangerous. In 1949, for example, UAW members found a bomb ticking behind the union's headquarters in Detroit.

For Walter and Victor, it was more personal. Both narrowly escaped being killed. In 1948, Walter was home in his kitchen. As he reached into the refrigerator for a bowl of peaches, someone fired a shotgun at him, blasting his right arm to pieces. Walter was in the hospital for weeks and had a cast on his arm for almost a year. Thirteen months later, in 1949, someone fired a shotgun at Victor as he was reading a newspaper in the living room of his home. He was hit in the face, throat, and shoulder, and the doctors who saved his life had to remove his right eyeball. They never learned who tried to kill them, but Walter and Victor were tough and they continued their work with the UAW.

Under Walter's leadership, by the 1960s the UAW was active in politics beyond the factory. Walter and his brothers had long believed that, in a democratic nation like the United States, unions could improve the lives of all people, not just union members. They believed that unions should also support freedom of speech, work to improve housing and health care, try to help the poor, and end discrimination against women, immigrants, and African Americans in the United States.

Walter became one of the most influential labor leaders in America. His speeches and ideas were printed in newspapers and magazines around the nation and world. Walter and his brothers met leaders of nations and unions from around the world. Under his direction, the UAW supported the Civil Rights movement, giving support and money to such civil rights leaders as Martin Luther King Jr. American presidents met with Walter and listened to his ideas; he was a close advisor to President Lyndon B. Johnson.

Victor, Roy, and Walter at a UAW meeting, 1949.

U.S. President John F. Kennedy and Walter at the 1962 UAW convention.

Dr. Martin Luther King Jr. and Walter *(far right)* making their way to the podium on the steps of the Lincoln Memorial during the Freedom March in Washington, D.C., on August 28, 1963.

The Reuther brothers suffered a great loss in 1968 when Roy died suddenly of a heart attack. This was a sad time for Walter and Victor. They mourned the loss of Roy, as did the entire membership of the UAW.

A great tragedy occurred in 1970, when Walter, May, and three other people died in a plane crash. They were on their way to Black Lake in northern Michigan, where the UAW was building a recreation and education center for its members. The plane carrying Walter and May came in too low for a landing, hit some trees, and burst into flames. Everyone in the plane was killed.

Walter and May's death was not only a shock to Victor and the Reuther family, it was an international incident. Their funeral was huge. Over three thousand people attended it, including dignitaries from around the world. UAW members around the nation mourned the loss of their leader.

Victor was devastated. He had lost another brother and his best friend. Two years later, he retired from the UAW to write a book about his life with Walter, Roy, and the Reuther family. The Reuther brothers' careers in the UAW had come to an end.

Epilogue

The Reuther brothers made a difference. They were determined to make a difference by improving the lives of working Americans, and this goal guided the brothers throughout their extraordinary lives. As leaders of the UAW, the brothers helped build the union into a powerful voice for its members, powerful enough to fight for and gain better wages, working conditions, and dignity in the workplace. They did indeed improve the lives of millions of American workers, and their ideas still influence labor unions in the United States today.

In many ways, however, the Reuther brothers were just ordinary Americans. They were the sons of immigrants who had come to the United States to make better lives for themselves. Like many other Americans, they had experienced hard times while growing up, especially when their father could not work.

The Reuther brothers were keen observers of the world around them. They saw the tremendous poverty caused by the Great Depression in America, and witnessed the loss of democracy in Germany and Russia. Most of all, they were deeply affected by the poor working conditions and the lack of dignity that factory workers experienced around the world.

The Reuther brothers were extraordinary. From humble beginnings, they rose to become leaders in the UAW and helped make it one of the most powerful and influential unions in the world. Walter, the most famous brother, is now recognized as one of the greatest labor union leaders in American history. With the support of Victor and Roy, he cre-

Left to right: Victor, Anna, Walter, Valentine, and Roy about 1955.

ated the goals and ideas that still guide the UAW today. Through their dedicated work, the Reuther brothers helped shape modern America.

GLOSSARY

apprentice: *(noun)* someone who learns a skill or trade by working for a skilled worker.

aptitude: *(noun)* a natural ability or talent.

assassination: *(noun)* the act of murder in a sudden attack, often for political reasons.

assemble: *(verb)* to fit or put together the parts of something.

assembly line: *(noun)* a factory system designed to save time and training. In many factories, the job of making a product such as a car is divided into many smaller jobs. Each worker is given one part to fit onto every item (car) made. While the product passes slowly by on a moving belt, the worker stays in same place, attaching his or her piece to the product as it goes by.

bargaining: *(verb)* to talk over a contract or a deal, trying to get the best possible terms.

boarder: *(noun)* a person who lives in another person's home for pay.

boarding house: *(noun)* a house in which one pays for a room and daily meals.

communism: *(noun)* a system of politics or economics in which the production of goods is owned by the community or the state, and there is no private ownership of businesses.

communist: *(noun)* a person who supports communism.

culture: *(noun)* the customs, beliefs, arts, and institutions of a group of people.

debate: *(verb)* to discuss or argue for or against an issue in an organized manner; *(noun)* the formal or organized discussion of an issue.

democratic: *(adjective)* having to do with a system of politics based on the idea of government by the people and equal rights for all.

depression: *(noun)* a time when there is less business activity and many people lose their jobs.

dictator: *(noun)* a ruler who has complete power over the government of a country.

economics: *(noun)* the science that deals with money, goods, and services and how they are related to one another.

factory: *(noun)* a building or group of buildings where things (products) are made.

foreign: *(adjective)* from a different country or place.

frugal: *(adjective)* careful not to waste money.

immigrant: *(noun)* someone who comes to live in a country in which he or she was not born.

industry: *(noun)* the overall activities and business involved in the manufacture of goods.

labor union: *(noun)* a group of workers joined together to protect and advance their interests.

manufacture: *(verb)* to make a product, especially through the use of machinery.

Nazi: *(noun)* a member or supporter of the political party that ruled Germany under Adolf Hitler from 1933 to 1945.

organize: *(verb)* to persuade employees to join a labor union.

peasant: *(noun)* someone who belongs to the group of small farmers and farm workers in Europe.

politics: *(noun)* the management or activities of government.

poverty: *(noun)* the condition of being poor.

racist: *(adjective)* a person who believes that one race of people is better than another.

revolution: *(noun)* the overthrow of a government.

strike: *(noun)* a stopping of work by employees in order to get better working conditions.

technology: *(noun)* the use of scientific knowledge in industry.

trade: *(noun)* a kind of work, especially one that involves skill with the hands.

trade union: *(noun)* workers in the same trade joined together to protect their interests.

tradition: *(noun)* ideas, customs, and beliefs that have been passed down from one generation to the next.

union: *(noun)* a group of workers who join together to protect their interests and improve their working conditions.

ACKNOWLEDGMENTS

A book is never the work of authors alone, and a number of people have assisted us along the way. We are extremely grateful and honored to have received suggestions, comments, and support from so many.

First, this book is the result of an idea from the associate director of the Wayne State University Press, Alice Nigoghosian, who took a deep and guiding interest in our work from start to finish. Thanks a million, Alice. Our book was greatly enhanced by the careful, thoughtful work of our editors at the Wayne State University Press, Kathy Wildfong and Sonia Benson. We also wish to thank the outside readers who read the initial manuscript and offered many valuable suggestions.

In writing this book, we also engaged many friends. Dr. Tony Carew helped shape our perspective on the Reuther brothers with his close reading of our manuscript, and through our reading of his excellent book on Walter Reuther. Our good friend Joe Turrini also provided insight and comments. We would also like to thank former UAW president Doug Fraser and former UAW vice president Millie Jeffrey for their generosity and suggestions. Millie's eleven-year-old niece, the very thoughtful and intelligent Kate Granholm Mulhern, also read our manuscript and provided us with helpful remarks.

Most of all, we would like to thank our family for their loving support, and for bearing with us during two years of discussions regarding this book. Kathy Duchene, Mike's sister, read our manuscript and provided helpful comments. Penny

Hardy, Pam's sister, was intimately involved in the shaping of chapter titles and themes. Two dear nieces were, perhaps, our greatest resources. Jackie Duchene, ten years old when she read several drafts of our manuscript, raised crucial questions that only someone her age could and also—to our chagrin— pointed out stylistic problems that left her unsettled. Finally, our niece Jennie Hardy, a teacher at Rudyard Middle School in the town of Rudyard in Michigan's upper peninsula, not only gave us her own precious advice, but allowed her sixth grade class to evaluate two early drafts of some chapters of the book. We thank, therefore, the members of Ms. Jennie Hardy's 1999–2000 class: Jennifer A., Jaimie C., Jim E., Bobby F., Danny F., Jordan G., John H., Chris H., Adam I., Tanya L., Elizabeth M., Alex M., Alyson N., Lisa O., Tom P., Tyler R., Travis S., Austin S., Ashley T. Dan V., and Alyse W. Many thanks to all who helped us.

We also hope this book honors the Reuther brothers, who made such a positive difference in the lives of so many working people. It is a great story that reflects the historical experience of many American families and a story that children should know.